Published by Amara Hospice Care for our clients and their families

A Legacy Keepsake

NAME _____

DATE _____

FACILITATED WITH THE HELP OF

AMARA

HOSPICE CARE

Life is made up of
experiences, family, friends,
accomplishments, and memories.

I want to share those that I cherish with my
loved ones and with generations to come.

The memories and messages I have
recorded here with the help of
Amara Hospice Care will be a gift from
me to you. May this gift draw you closer to
our family as you share it, and may my
family enjoy the words and wonder it
holds for years to come.

THE BEGINNING

My father's full name: _____

Father's place of birth: _____

Father's date of birth: _____

My mother's maiden name: _____

Mother's place of birth: _____

Mother's date of birth: _____

Parents' place of marriage: _____

Parents' date of marriage: _____

My place of marriage: _____

"To us, family means putting your arms around each other and being there." *Barbara Bush*

My date of marriage:_____

My paternal grandparents: _____

My maternal grandparents: _____

My full given name: _____

My siblings:_____

My place of birth: _____

My date of birth: _____

Where I grew up:_____

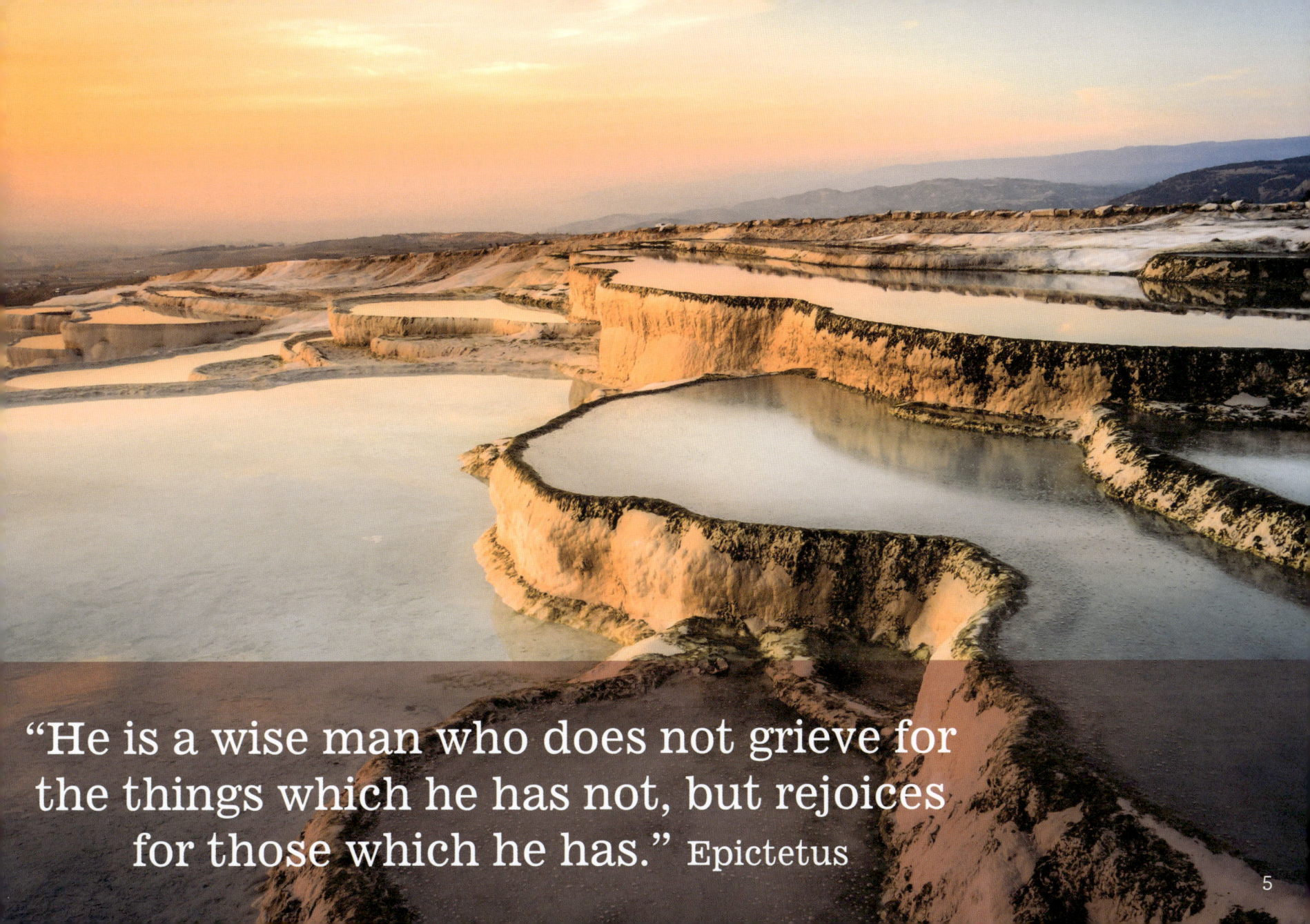

"He is a wise man who does not grieve for the things which he has not, but rejoices for those which he has." Epictetus

notes

The Way It Was

"Childhood is the most beautiful of all life's seasons." Author Unknown

8

CHILDHOOD

Describe your childhood home. _____

_____

_____

_____

Did you have any special interests or talents as a child?_____

_____

Did you take lessons of any kind? _____

_____

Were you part of a club, troop or other organization? _____

_____

"Having a two-year-old is like having a blender that you don't have the top for." Jerry Seinfeld

What do you remember about your group? _____

_____

_____

_____

Did you participate in sports? _____

Which sports and until what age did you play? _____

_____

_____

favorite recipes

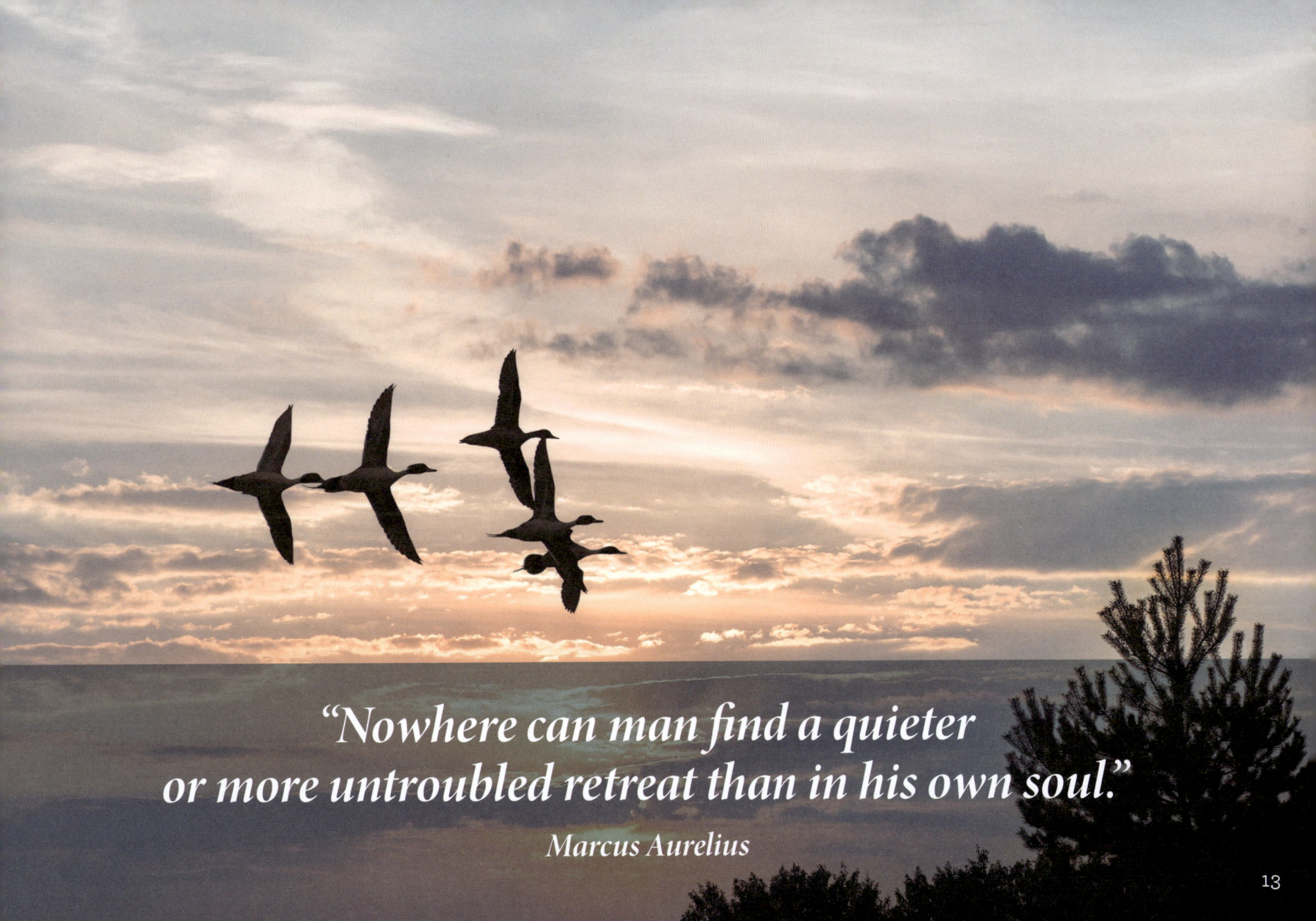

"*Nowhere can man find a quieter or more untroubled retreat than in his own soul.*"

Marcus Aurelius

FAMILY LIFE

What was your mother like when you were young? _____

_____

_____

Did she work outside the home? _____

How would you finish this sentence, "One thing my mom always said was ..."? _____

_____

What is your favorite memory of your mother? _____

_____

_____

In what ways are you like your mother? _____

_____

_____

What was your father like when you were young?_____

_____

_____

His appearance and manner?_____

_____

How would you finish this sentence, "One thing my dad always said was..."?_____

_____

"I remember my mother's prayers and they have always followed me. They have clung to me all my life." *Abraham Lincoln*

"When you look at your life, the greatest happinesses are family happinesses." *Joyce Brothers*

What did you most enjoy doing with your father?_____

_____

_____

What is a favorite memory of your father?_____

_____

_____

How are you like your father?_____

_____

_____

EDUCATION

Schools I attended:

Grammar School: _____

High School: _____

What did you enjoy most about school? _____

_____

_____

Favorite subject: _____

"If you can find a path with no obstacles, it probably doesn't lead anywhere." *Frank A. Clark*

College: _____

_____

Did you pursue a specific degree? _____

Why was it important to you?_____

_____

_____

"The way a team plays as a whole determines its success. You may have the greatest bunch of individual stars in the world, but if they don't play together, the club won't be worth a dime." Babe Ruth

23

My military record:

Conflict or War: _____ Branch:_____

Enlistment date and place: _____

Time in service: _____

Military ID: _____

History of service: _____

_____

_____

_____

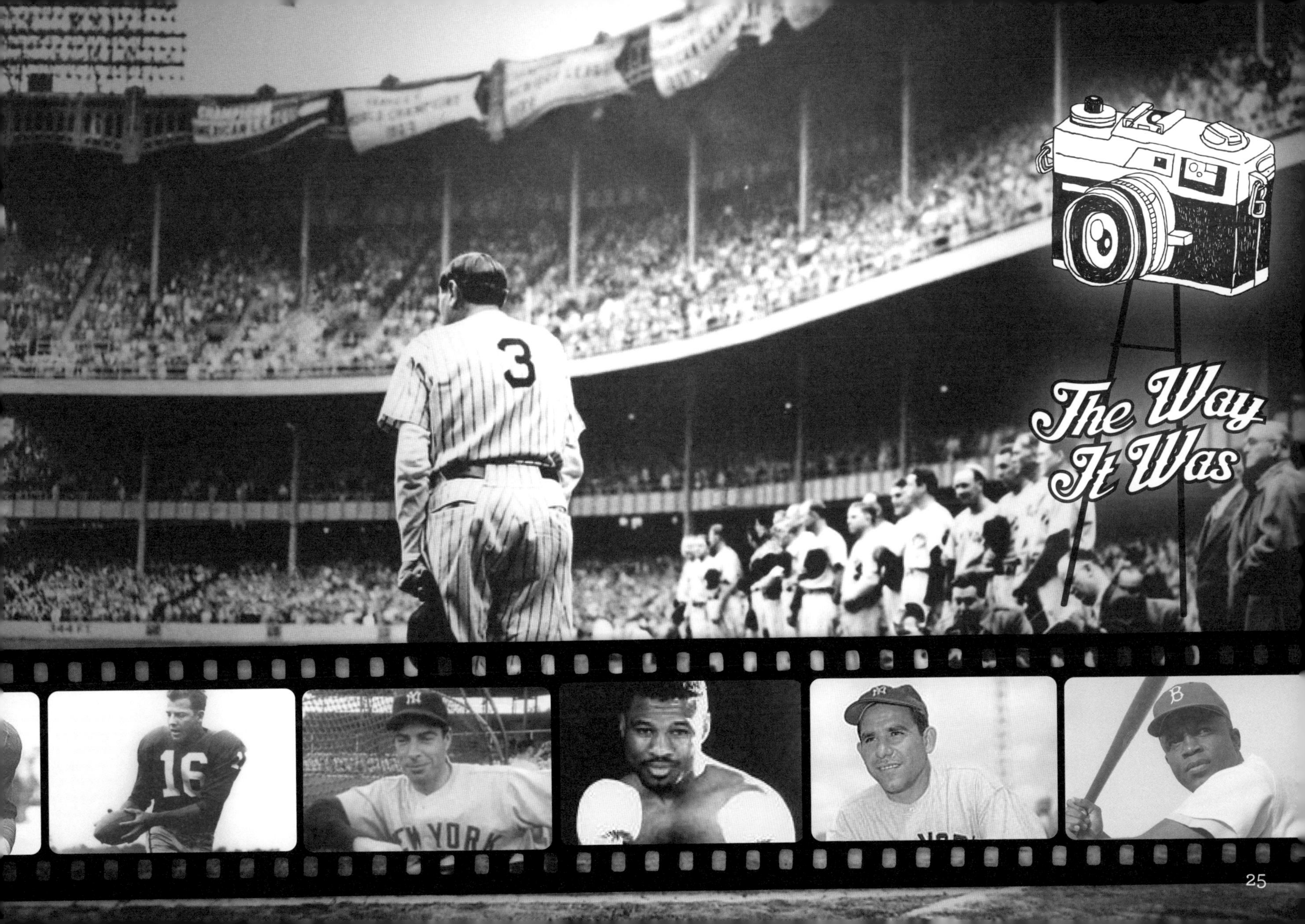

"Heaven knows we need never be ashamed of our tears, for they are rain upon the blinding dust of earth, overlying our hard hearts." *Charles Dickens*

26

REFLECTION

Do you have a favorite song? _____

Why is this song special to you? _____

_____

_____

Is there a television show you most enjoy? _____

Why is it a favorite? _____

_____

_____

What were your goals and aspirations after high school? _____

_____

_____

_____

How old were you when you moved away from home? _____

What was your first place like? _____

_____

_____

_____

_____

"*Forgive, not because they deserve forgiveness, but because you deserve peace.*"
Author Unknown

notes

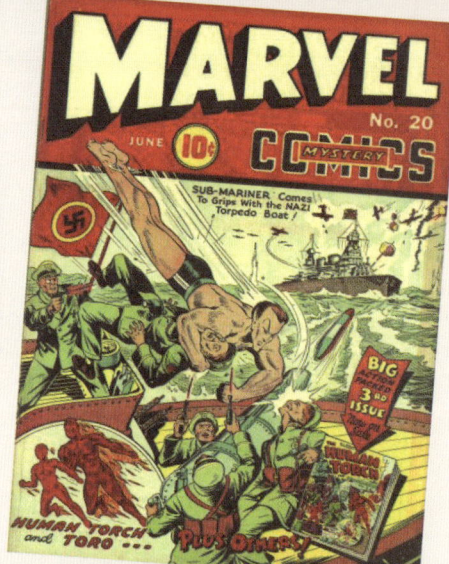

The Way It Was

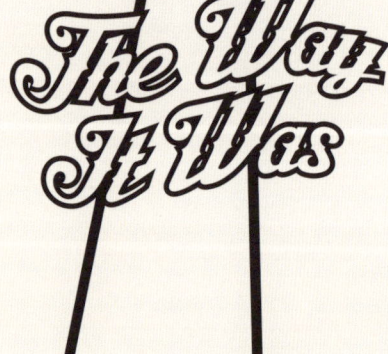

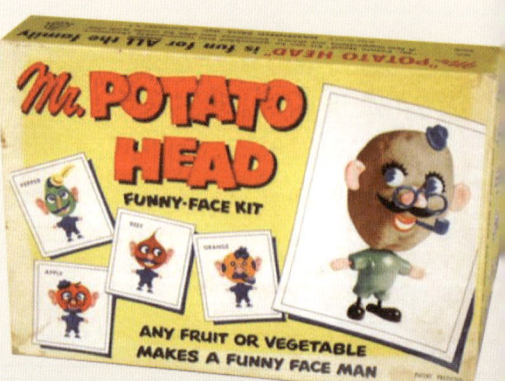

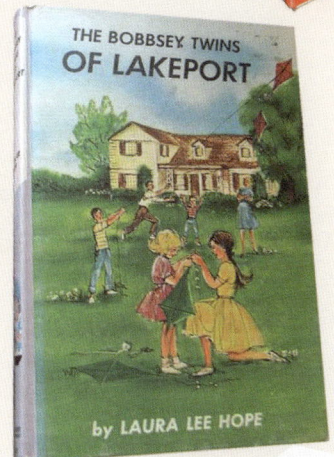

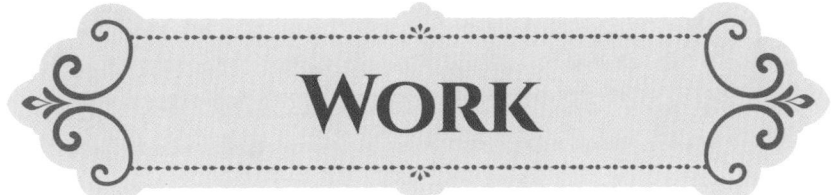

WORK

What was your first job? _____

_____

What was the pay? _____

How did you get it? _____

_____

_____

_____

_____

_____

"Wrinkles should merely indicate where smiles have been." Mark Twain

What led you to your line of work?

_____

_____

_____

_____

_____

_____

_____

"There is no such thing in anyone's life as an unimportant day." Alexander Woollcott

37

LOVE AND MARRIAGE

How old were you when you met your spouse? _____

How did you meet? _____

_____

_____

What was the attraction? _____

_____

_____

What did you enjoy doing together? _____

_____

_____

"True love stories never have endings." Richard Bach

Describe the marriage proposal. _____

_____

_____

_____

Where and when were you married? _____

_____

_____

Where did you go on your honeymoon? _____

Recall a special moment or event from your trip._____

_____

_____

Where did you live after you got married?_____

What activities have you and your spouse enjoyed together?_____

_____

_____

What do you think is most important in maintaining a healthy marriage? _____

_____

_____

_____

_____

Photos and Memorabilia

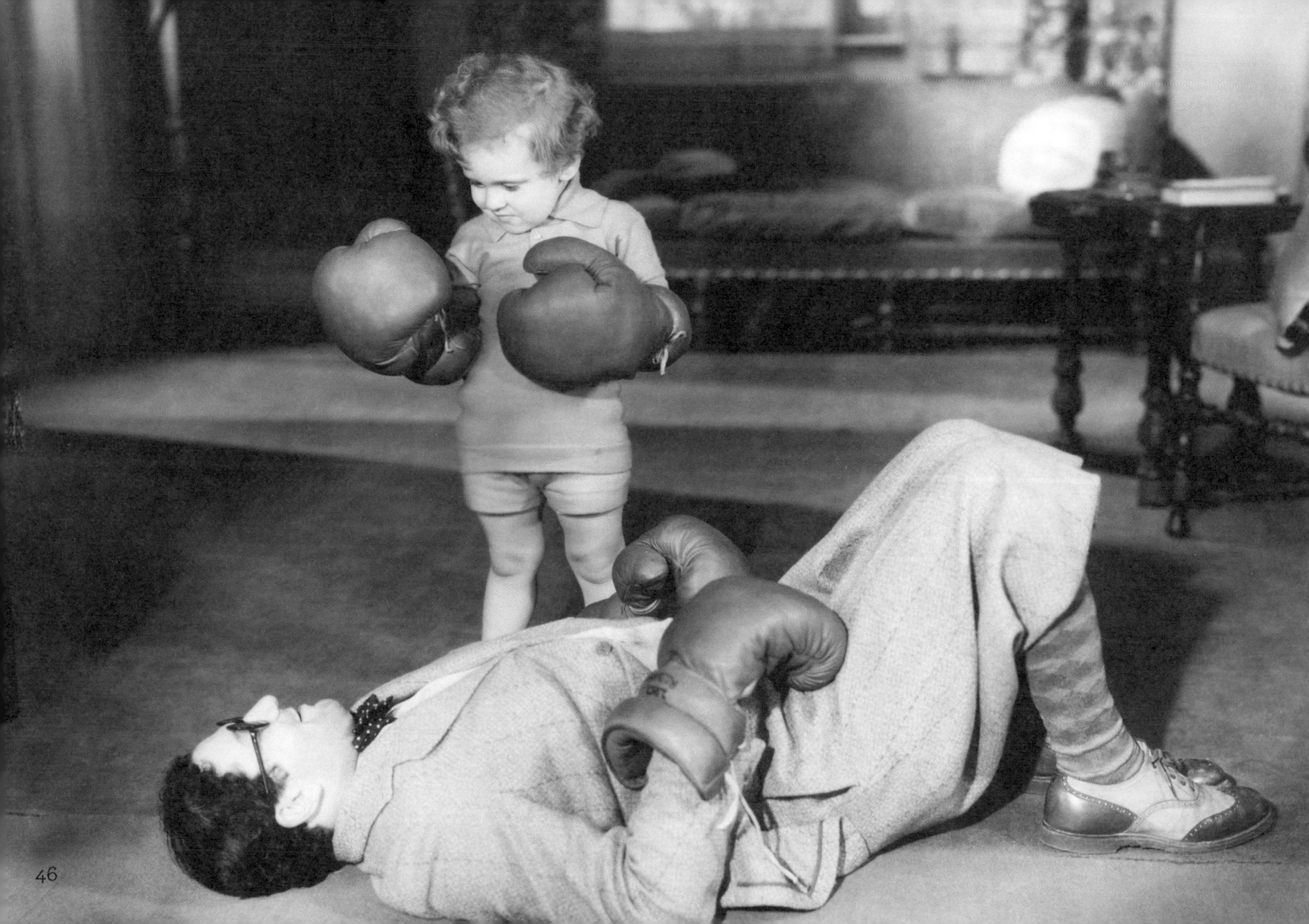

PARENTHOOD

Do your children's names have a special meaning, or are they named after a special person? _____

_____

_____

_____

What activities did you most enjoy doing with your children? _____

_____

_____

_____

"Children make your life important."
Erma Bombeck

What similarities do you see between yourself or your spouse and your children? _____

_____

_____

_____

What values did you try to nurture in your children? _____

_____

_____

_____

"A man is not where he lives, but where he loves." *Latin Proverb*

What has been your greatest joy in being a parent? _____

_____

_____

What are things you hope your children have learned from you?_____

_____

_____

Is there a special message you have for your children?_____

_____

_____

"When we are no longer able to change a situation, we are challenged to change ourselves."

Viktor Frankl

notes

CELEBRATIONS

What holidays did your family enjoy celebrating? _____

_____

_____

_____

_____

What holiday traditions from your childhood did you pass on to your children?_____

_____

_____

_____

_____

"If the only prayer you said in your whole life was, 'thank you', that would suffice."

Meister Eckhart

Where did the tradition originate? _____

_____

_____

_____

_____

_____

_____

The Way It Was

"*I simply believe that some part of the human self or soul is not subject to the laws of space and time.*" Carl Jung

LIFE EVENTS

What was the happiest time of your life? _____

_____

_____

_____

_____

_____

_____

_____

_____

"Once you find someone to share your ups and downs, downs are almost as good as ups." Robert Brault

What was the saddest? _____

_____

_____

_____

_____

_____

_____

_____

Photos and Memorabilia

The Way It Was

notes

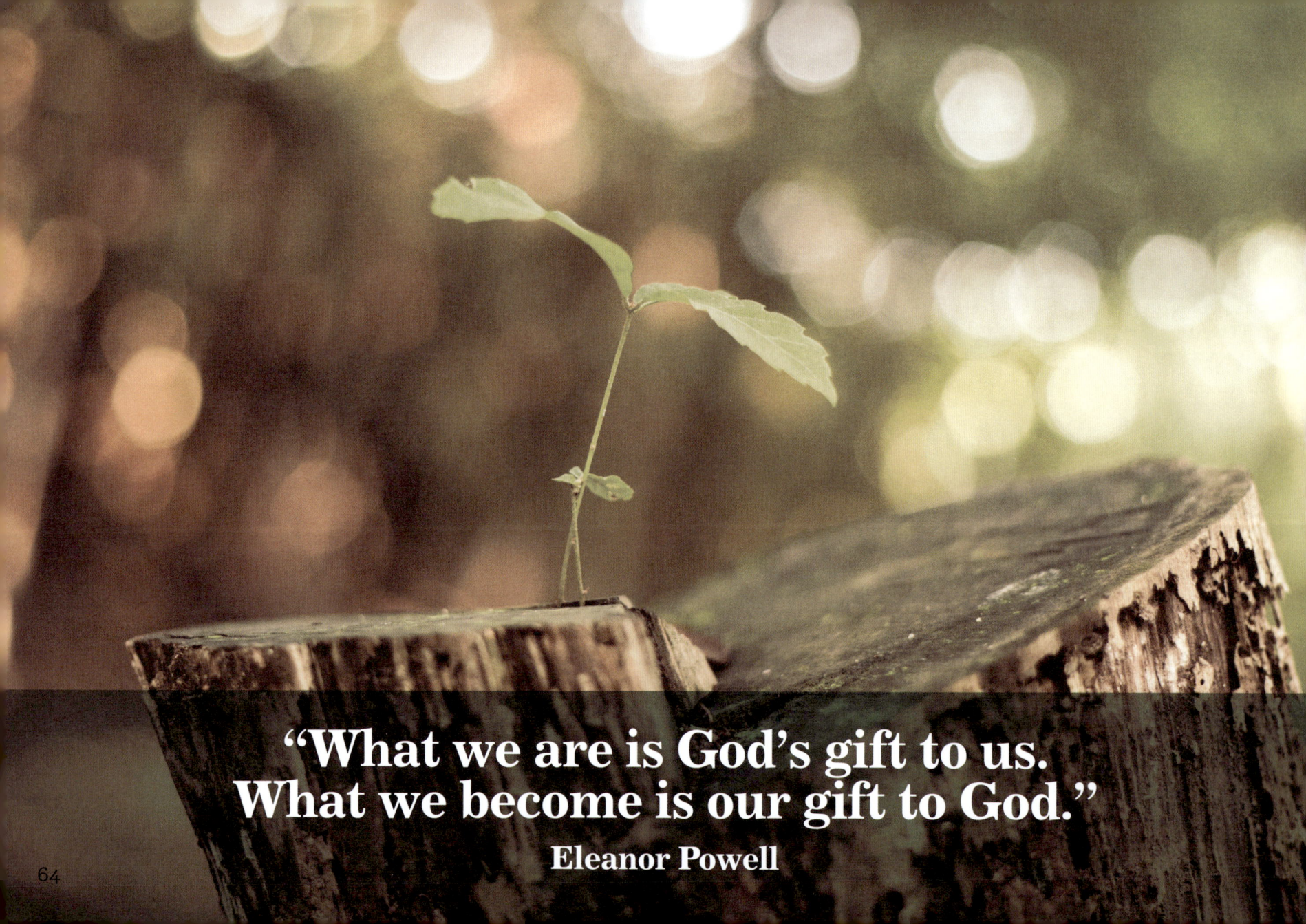

"What we are is God's gift to us.
What we become is our gift to God."

Eleanor Powell

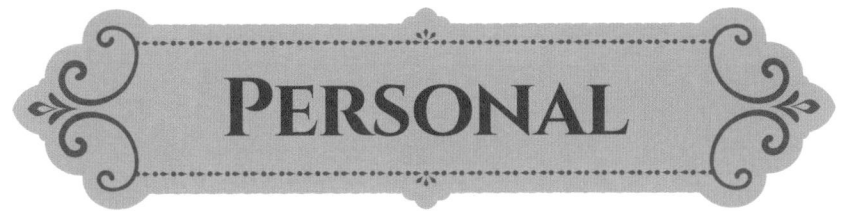

PERSONAL

What is the most fun, interesting, or exciting place you've ever visited? _____

_____

_____

Have you ever dedicated yourself to a cause or organization? Why was it important to you?_____

_____

_____

What did you accomplish that you are especially proud of? _____

_____

"If you want others to be happy, practice compassion. If you want to be happy, practice compassion." Dalai Lama

What is one thing you would never change about the way you've lived your life? _____

_____

_____

_____

What is one thing you wish you had done differently? _____

_____

_____

_____

favorite jokes

"Laughter is the sunbeam of the soul." *Thomas Mann*

"Nobody has ever measured, even poets, how much a heart can hold."
Zelda Fitzgerald

What are your hopes for your family? _____

_____

_____

_____

_____

The Way It Was

"Too often we underestimate the power of a touch, a smile, a kind word, a listening ear, an honest compliment, or the smallest act of caring, all of which have the potential to turn a life around."
Leo Buscaglia

INSPIRATION

Who has made the greatest impact on your life? _____

_____

_____

_____

_____

What role does religion or spirituality play in your life? Has this changed over the years? _____

_____

_____

_____

_____

"The difference between try and triumph is a little umph."
Author Unknown

What in your life are you most thankful for? _____

_____

_____

_____

_____

What is the most important thing that you have learned in life? _____

_____

_____

_____

_____

"Who does not
thank for
little will not
thank for much."
Estonian Proverb

What advice would you give future generations of your family? _____

_____

_____

_____

Any other favorite memories, stories or messages?_____

_____

_____

_____

Inspirational saying, poem, or thought: _____

_____

_____

_____

May you always have work for your hands to do.

May your pockets hold always a coin or two.

May the sun shine bright on your windowpane.

May the rainbow be certain to follow each rain.

May the hand of a friend always be near you.

And may God fill your heart with gladness to cheer you.

Irish Blessing

Genetics...

Genetics helps to give us a better understanding of ourselves. The knowledge of our own genetics helps us to treat diseases before they occur. Illnesses relating to genetics experienced in my family by spouse, siblings, grandparents, aunts or uncles, that I am aware of include:

DISEASE	FAMILY MEMBER(S)	DISEASE	FAMILY MEMBER(S)
Alzheimer's Disease	_____	Cancer of _____	_____
ALS	_____	Cancer of _____	_____
Anemia	_____	Cerebral Vascular Disease	_____
Asthma	_____	Coronary Artery Disease	_____
Arthritis	_____	Congenital Heart Disease	_____
Bleeding Disorders	_____	Cystic Fibrosis	_____
Bone Diseases	_____	Dementia	_____
Brain Diseases	_____	Diabetes	_____
Cancer of _____	_____	Diverticulitis	_____
Cancer of _____	_____	Dwarfism	_____

DISEASE	FAMILY MEMBER(S)	DISEASE	FAMILY MEMBER(S)
Gangrene	_____	Restless Leg Syndrome	_____
Gastrointestinal Disorders	_____	Rheumatoid Arthritis	_____
Heart Disease	_____	Sickle Cell Anemia	_____
Hemophilia	_____	Spinal Disorders	_____
Huntington's Disease	_____	Stroke	_____
Hypertension	_____	Thyroid Disease	_____
Kidney Disease	_____	Wilson's Disease	_____
Leukemia	_____	Other_____	_____
Lung Disorders	_____	Other_____	_____
Lymphoma	_____	Other_____	_____
Muscular Dystrophy	_____	Other_____	_____
PKU	_____	Other_____	_____